ROSS RICHIE CEO & Founder • MARK SMYLIE Founder of Archaia • MATT GAGNON Editor-in-Chief • FILIP SABLIK VP of Publishing & Marketing • STEPHEN CHRISTY VP of Development
LANCE KREITER VP of Licensing & Merchandising • PHIL BARBARO VP of Finance • BRYCE CARLSON Managing Editor • MEL CAYLO Marketing Manager • SCOTT NEWMAN Production Design Manager
IRENE BRADISH Operations Manager • CHRISTINE DINH Brand Communications Manager • DAFNA PLEBAN Editor • SHANNON WATTERS Editor • ERIC HARBURN Editor • REBECCA TAYLOR Editor
IAN BRILL Editor • CHRIS ROSA Assistant Editor • ALEX GALER Assistant Editor • WHITNEY LEOPARD Assistant Editor • JASMINE AMIRI Assistant Editor • CAMERON CHITTOCK Assistant Editor
KELSEY DIETERICH Production Designer • EMI YONEMURA BROWN Production Designer • DEVIN FUNCHES E-Commerce & Inventory Coordinator • ANDY LIEGL Event Coordinator • BRIANNA HART Executive Assistant
AARON FERRARA Operations Assistant • JOSÉ MEZA Sales Assistant • MICHELLE ANKLEY Sales Assistant • ELIZABETH LOUGHRIDGE Accounting Assistant • STEPHANIE HOCUTT PR Assistant

REGULAR SHOW™

VOLUME ONE

REGULAR

CREATED BY JG QUINTEL

WRITTEN BY **KC GREEN**

ART BY **ALLISON STREJLAU**

COLORS BY **LISA MOORE**

LETTERS BY **STEVE WANDS**

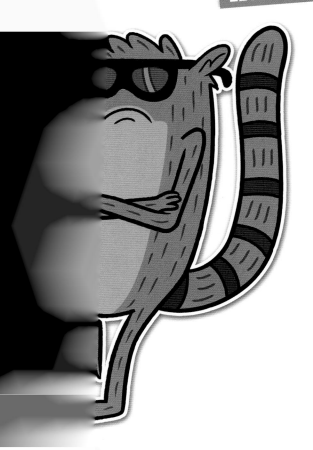

COVER BY

CHRIS HOUGHTON

ASSISTANT EDITOR

WHITNEY LEOPARD

EDITOR

SHANNON WATTERS

DESIGNER

HANNAH NANCE PARTLOW

SHOW™

WITH SPECIAL THANKS TO MARISA MARIONAKIS, RICK BLANCO,
CURTIS LELASH, LAURIE HALAL-ONO, AND THE WONDERFUL
FOLKS AT CARTOON NETWORK.

THIS
BLOWS.

BECAUSE YOU CAN'T BE TRUSTED WITH ANYTHING ELSE.
NOT EVEN GETTING WATER FOR THE TALENT?
THOMAS IS ALREADY ON TOP OF THAT.
BUT I KNOOOWW *COUGH COUGH COUGH COUGH COUGH* AAAA...
I KNOOOOWWW--

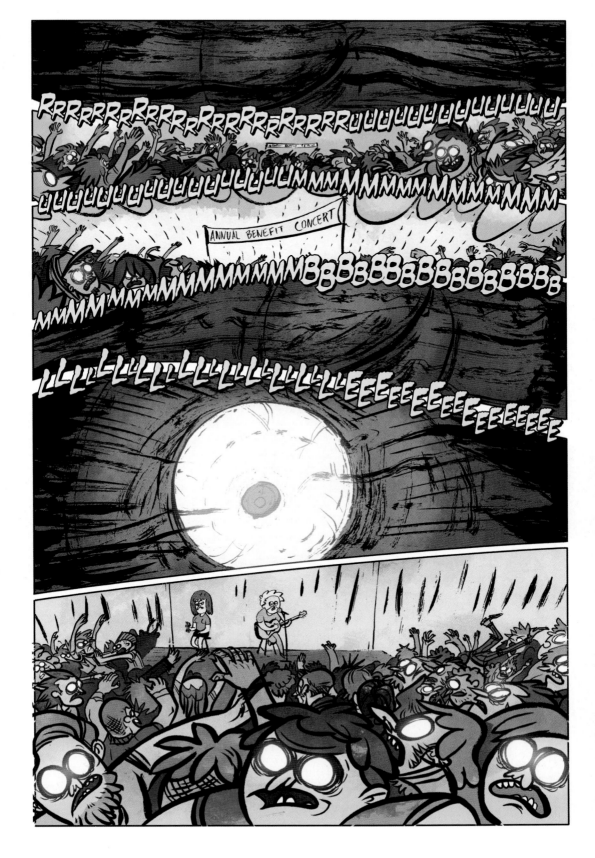

HOLY CRAP, DUDE!

I'VE SEEN THIS BEFORE! WHEN A MOSH PIT IS STARTED WHERE NO MOSH PIT SHOULD EVER BE, IT CAN OPEN A RIFT BETWEEN MUSIC GENRES!

THERE IS MENTION OF A **DARK FORCE** WHO FEEDS OFF OF THE ROWDY ENERGY OF YOUNG ADOLESCENTS. HE SLEEPS BELOW THE PARK...FOREVER DORMANT...

MUSCLE MAN STARTING THAT MOSH PIT MUST HAVE--

EXACTLY. **THE BEAST** HAS BEEN AWOKEN BY MUSCLE MAN'S EXCESSIVE ROWDINESS. ITS **DARK POWER** IS LEAKING OUT OF THE EARTH, AFFECTING ALL THESE PEOPLE.

SO HOW DO WE STOP THIS, SKIPS?

BE CAREFUL, NOW!!

AND BE QUICK ABOUT IT!!

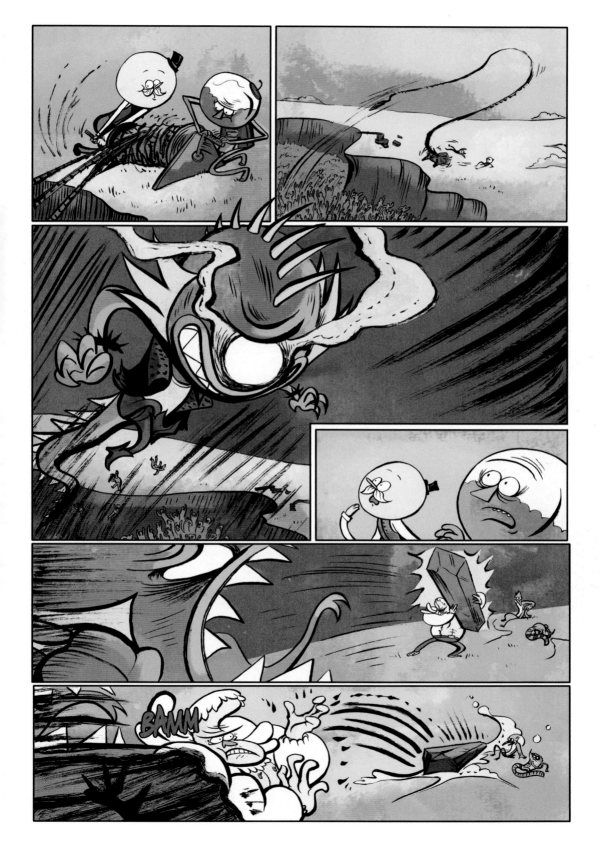

AW, MAN...THIS CONCERT MUST HAVE SUCKED SO MUCH THAT I CAN'T REMEMBER ANYTHING.

I HOPE I DIDN'T MAKE ANY CHOICES THAT I'M GOING TO REGRET FOR THE REST OF MY LIFE...

BOOO!

BOOO!

LAME!

END.

GIVE IT UP, DUDE! *I DON'T THINK THERE IS ANYONE ELSE WORSE AT BALANCING THE RAKE THAN YOU.*

WHATCHA DOIN', LADIES? BALANCING THE RAKE, HUH? *LET ME AT IT, BROS!!*

YEAH, LIKE YOU COULD DO ANY BETTER...

YOU KNOW WHO ELSE LOVES TO BALANCE RAKES!!? MY--

SNAP!

MMO--

LOOKS LIKE I STAND CORRECTED, RIGBY. MUSCLE MAN MIGHT BE WORSE AT BALANCING A RAKE THAN YOU ARE.

I JUST NEED ANOTHER GO AT IT!

THAT WAS THE ONLY RAKE WE HAVE LEFT AT THE PARK, MUSCLE MAN!

DID YOUR *MOM* NOT TEACH YOU HOW TO BALANCE A RAKE?

WEAUH...WELL SHE *DID* TEACH ME HOW TO CUT MY HAIR, YOU *JERK!*

DID I HEAR SOMEONE SAY HAIRCUT?

I USED TO CUT SKIPS' HAIR ALL THE TIME, YOU KNOW!

YOU KNOW HOW TO CUT HAIR?

WELL, I HAVEN'T DONE IT IN A WHILE, BUT IT'S LIKE RIDING A BIKE! YOU NEVER FORGET! AND I'D LOVE TO GIVE ANOTHER GO AT IT!!

IT HAS BEEN SO LONG SINCE I'VE GOTTEN OUT THE OLD TRIMMING SHEARS! PLEASE LET ME DO YOU A KINDNESS, PLEASE, MORDECAI.

COME, COME! THEY'RE UP IN MY ROOM!

WELL, SURE. WHY NOT? IT'LL SAVE ME SOME CASH FOR THE DATE.

ALL RIGHT!

WHAT ARE YOU DOING, RIGBY?

FIXING THE RAKE, SKIPS! WHAT'S IT LOOK LIKE?!

IT LOOKS LIKE YOU'RE DOING SOMETHING POORLY.

WHERE'S MORDECAI?

POPS IS GIVING HIM A HAIRCUT UPSTAIRS.

THEY WERE SO BAD I HAD TO *LIE* TO POPS TO STOP HIM FROM GIVING ME ANY MORE HAIRCUTS.

WHAT'D YOU TELL HIM?

I TOLD HIM MY HAIR NEVER GREW ANYMORE. HE SEEMED TO BUY IT, BUT I HAD TO BE VIGILANT ABOUT LETTING MY HAIR NEVER GROW PAST WHERE IT IS NOW.

AAAAHHHGHHHH

MORDECAI!

AH HA! YOU'RE ALL JUST IN TIME TO SCREAM IN JOY WITH US FOR MY NEWEST TRIUMPH!

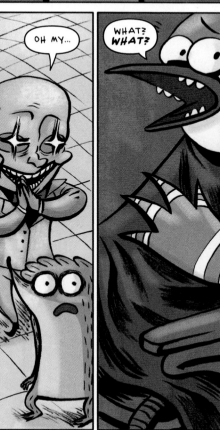

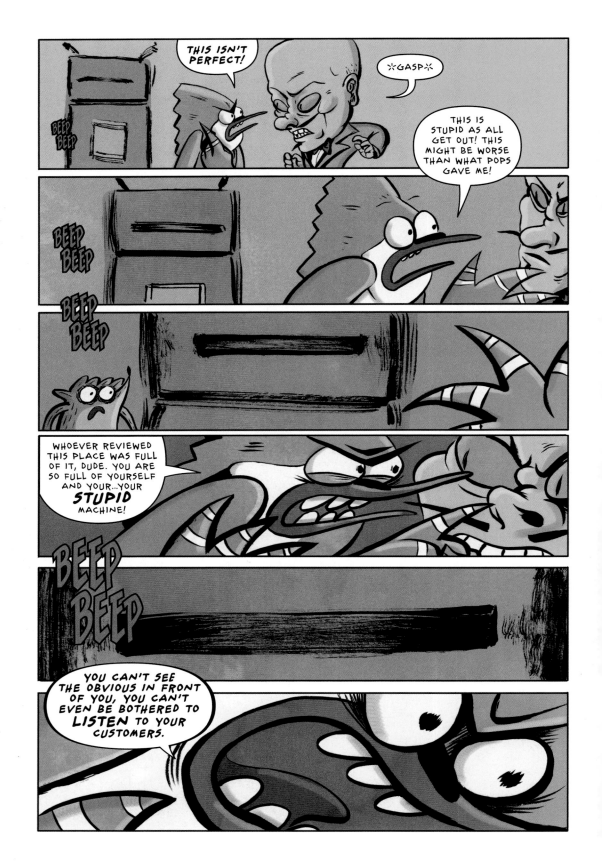

THE END.

SHORT STORIES, BRO

REGULAR SHOW

STORY + ART BY BRIAN BUTLER   COLOR BY MAARTA LAIHO

WIDE AWAKE

SWOO!

WORDS AND COLORS BY
SHAUN STEVEN STRUBLE

ILLUSTRATIONS BY
SINA GRACE

IT WAS PRETTY COOL OF BENSON TO GIVE US TOMORROW OFF SO THAT WE CAN GO TO THE TRI-COUNTY COMIC EXPO.

SH'YEAH, RIGHT.

HE MADE US DO THREE TIMES THE WORK WE'D HAVE DONE TOMORROW --

ON TOP OF OUR CHORES FOR TODAY.

YEAH.

BUT NOW, AT LEAST, WE'LL BE FIRST IN LINE TO MEET TV'S DANNY REINHOFF, STAR OF *LETHAL DRIVER COP!*

OH CRAP, DUDE.

IS THAT THE TIME?

THERE'S NO WAY WE'LL MAKE IT IN TIME IF WE SLEEP. DANNY REINHOFF IS ONLY SIGNING FROM 7 TO 9. WHAT IF WE OVERSLEEP?

DON'T WORRY ABOUT IT, MAN.

WE'LL JUST STAY UP ALL NIGHT, GO TO THE SIGNING IN THE MORNING AND CATCH A NAP AFTERWARDS.

IT'LL BE *EASY.*

I DON'T KNOW, RIGBY.

I'VE SEEN YOU FALL ASLEEP ON OUR LUNCH BREAK.

COME ON, MORDECAI. YOU JUST GOTTA KNOW THE RIGHT TECHNIQUES.

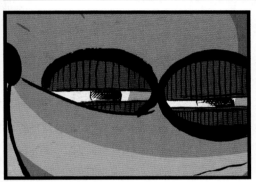

04:44AM

MY EYES!

EXCUSE ME...

SWITCH!

HEY, YOU LOOK TIRED.

YOU GUYS REALLY SHOULD GO TO SLEEP.

IS THAT A DUDE MADE OUT OF PILLOWS?

I THINK THAT'S THE SANDMAN, DUDE.

WHAT?

HE JUST LOOKS LIKE A LAME DUDE MADE OUT OF PILLOWS.

HE'S GOING TO TRY AND MAKE US SLEEP.

DUDE, GET LOST BEFORE WE CALL THE COPS.

YEAH! AND STAY OUT!

SERIOUSLY GUYS...

YOU SHOULD TAKE A NAP. I PROMISE I WON'T STEAL ANYTHING.

YAWN!

HEY, MORDECAI.

YOU STILL AWAKE?

BARELY.

JUST ONE MORE HOUR AND THEN WE GET TO MEET THE STAR OF THE BEST COP SHOW OF ALL TIME.

"THIS TIME, THE CAR IS GETTING TOO OLD FOR THIS."

FWOOF!

GO... TO... SLEEP!

DUDE.

WE SAID STAY OUT!

WHA?!

RIGBY, THE LOUD MUSIC IS WEAKENING HIM.

YOU KNOW WHAT THAT MEANS, RIGHT?

HMM HMM HMM!!!

HERE.

HOLD THIS.

FWOOF!

OOOOOOOOOOOH

AND JUST IN TIME, TOO!

WE CAN JUST MAKE IT TO THE SIGNING!

WHAT THE--?!

YOU TWO ARE NOT GOING ANYWHERE UNTIL YOU CLEAN UP THIS MESS!

END.

HAPPY BIRTHDAY RIGBY!

IT'S MY... BIRTHDAY?

HOW COULD YOU FORGET YOUR OWN BIRTHDAY, GENIUS? DON'S BEEN PLANNING THIS WITH ME AND EILEEN FOR MONTHS!

YOU GUYS DID ALL THIS... **FOR ME?**

WHY DO YOU THINK I MADE YOU WEAR THE HELMET? **IN CASE WE RAN INTO THEM!**

OF COURSE BRO! I THINK YOU KNOW WHAT WE WANT IN RETURN!

A THANK YOU CARD?

NO... A SUGARPILE!!!

HAPPY BIRTHDAY, RIGBY!

UM... OUR FACES ARE TOUCHING... AWKWARD!

END

REGGINS

BY
BRANDON T. SNIDER &
WOOK JIN CLARK

I'M FULL.

BUUURRRPPP

UGH, STOP WITH THOSE WARM BURPS. THEY'RE GROSS.

AND WHAT ARE YOU TALKING ABOUT? YOU BARELY ATE ANYTHING.

SO WHAT? I EAT WHAT I WANT, WHEN I WANT BECAUSE I'M

UNPREDICTABLE!

WHATEVER, DUDE. I GUESS YOU WON'T BE A MEMBER OF THE CLEAN PLATE CLUB THEN.

THERE'S A CLUB FOR CLEAN PLATES? I WANT IN! LET'S MEET TONIGHT AT SEVEN PM!

NO, RIGBY. IT'S JUST A TRICK THAT PARENTS PLAY ON THEIR KIDS TO GET THEM TO FINISH THEIR DINNER.

BESIDES, YOU'RE NOT A. . . PLATE.

OH. HA HA! I GET IT.

THAT'S HILARIOUS. NICE ONE, MORDECAI.

SO YOU'RE SAYING THERE'S NOT A CLUB?

NO CLUB.

RIGBY, YOU GOTTA STOP THROWING OUT PERFECTLY GOOD FOOD. IT'S A WASTE.

YOU'RE GONNA ATTRACT FREEGANS.

I PLAY BY MY OWN RULES.

BESIDES IT'S JUST FOOD. THERE'S SO MUCH OF IT.

FREEGANS? PSHAW!

I'M TOSSIN' IT, MAN. LET 'EM COME FOR ME!

MORDECAI, IF I POUR A BUNCH OF FOOD ON A PILE OF OLD FOOD WILL IT GROW NEW FOOD?

NO, DUDE.

YOU'RE REALLY GONNA DO IT, AREN'T YOU?!

GAH!!! MORDECAI!

THERE'S A SUNBURNT LEPRECHAUN IN THE TRASH!

RIGBY, GET IN THE HOUSE, NOW!

LATER

FREEGANS, DUDE! WE'VE GOT FREEGANS! YOU DID THIS, RIGBY!

I'M SORRY, MAN! WHAT DO WE DO? CAN WE SPRAY 'EM?! I CAN MAKE A SPRAY!

THERE COULD BE THOUSANDS OF THEM OUT THERE. I KNEW THIS WAS GONNA HAPPEN.

YOU AND YOUR DUMB FOOD HEAP! NOW WE'RE GONNA GET HANDED SOME COLD, HARD DINNER JUSTICE.

WHAT'S THAT?

DINNER JUSTICE PAYBACK FOR NOT FINISHING A DELICIOUS DINNER!

IS THERE BREAKFAST JUSTICE?

NO WAY. ARE YOU KIDDING ME? EVERYONE EATS ALL THEIR BREAKFAST ALL THE TIME.

TRUE DAT. SO WHAT DO WE DO?

IT'S THE MOST DELICIOUS MEAL OF THE DAY.

WE HAVE TO TRAP THEM. FIRST WE'LL NEED A NICE JUICY STEAK AND THEN MAYBE SOME FINGERLING POTATOES WITH WARM AU JUS AND—

RIGBY!!

I'M HERE! LET'S GET STEAK!?

EVEN LATER

OKAY SO ALL WE REALLY HAVE IS THIS CHEESE THAT EXPIRES NEXT WEEK.

LET'S MELT IT AND MAKE NACHOS.

AWWW YEAAAHUH!

FOCUS, RIGBY! WE'RE NOT MAKING MELTY CHEESE NACHOS EVEN THOUGH THAT SOUNDS PRETTY AWESOME RIGHT NOW.

WE PUT THIS BLOCK OUT THERE SO THEY'LL SEE THE DATE, GRAB IT AND GO MENTAL.

THAT'S WHEN WE SWOOP IN WITH SWEET NINJA MOVES AND THIS NET--

YOU THROWIN' THAT SWEET CHEESE OUT TOO? MAN, YOU GUYS ARE WASTEOIDS.

COOL FLOSS NET, THOUGH.

GAH! GET IT AWAY!

OUT FREEGAN! I CAST YOU OUT!

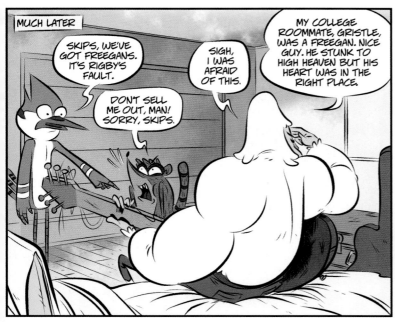

MUCH LATER

SKIPS, WE'VE GOT FREEGANS. IT'S RIGBY'S FAULT.

DON'T SELL ME OUT, MAN! SORRY, SKIPS.

SIGH, I WAS AFRAID OF THIS.

MY COLLEGE ROOMMATE, GRISTLE, WAS A FREEGAN. NICE GUY. HE STUNK TO HIGH HEAVEN BUT HIS HEART WAS IN THE RIGHT PLACE.

I THINK HE STILL OWES ME $20 TOO. ANYWAY, YOU HAVE TO TALK TO THESE GUYS ON THEIR LEVEL.

CAN'T SAY I DISAGREE WITH THEIR PHILOSOPHY.

YOU TWO HANG BACK AND LET ME HANDLE THIS.

THERE'S AN ITALIAN JOINT NEARBY CALLED MARIO'S. THEY MAKE A KILLER MEATBALL.

I'VE SEEN 'EM TOSS THE EXTRAS OUT AT NIGHT. WHY DON'T YOU GIVE 'EM SOME DINNER JUSTICE?

YOU'RE A GOOD YETI, SKIPS. THE BEST ONE I'VE EVER KNOWN.

YOU TOO, GRIS.

KEEP ON KEEPIN' ON, BROTHER.

LET'S ROLL!

RIGBY, NEVER WASTE THE FOOD YOU'RE GIVEN.

DON'T WORRY, SKIPS. I'VE SEEN THE LIGHT. CLEAN PLATE CLUB, HERE I COME!

A CLUB... FOR CLEAN PLATES? NOW I'VE HEARD EVERYTHING.

HEY SKIPS, DID YOU EVER GET THAT $20 THAT GRISTLE OWED YOU?

SIGH.

I'M JUST GONNA TOSS ALL THESE MEATBALLS OUT HERE INSTEAD OF GIVING THEM TO THAT HOMELESS SHELTER.

CAN YOU IMAGINE GIVING FINE MEATBALLS LIKE THESE AWAY FOR FREE?

HAHAHA!

FIN.

COVER GALLERY

ISSUE ONE Cover A
NICK EDWARDS

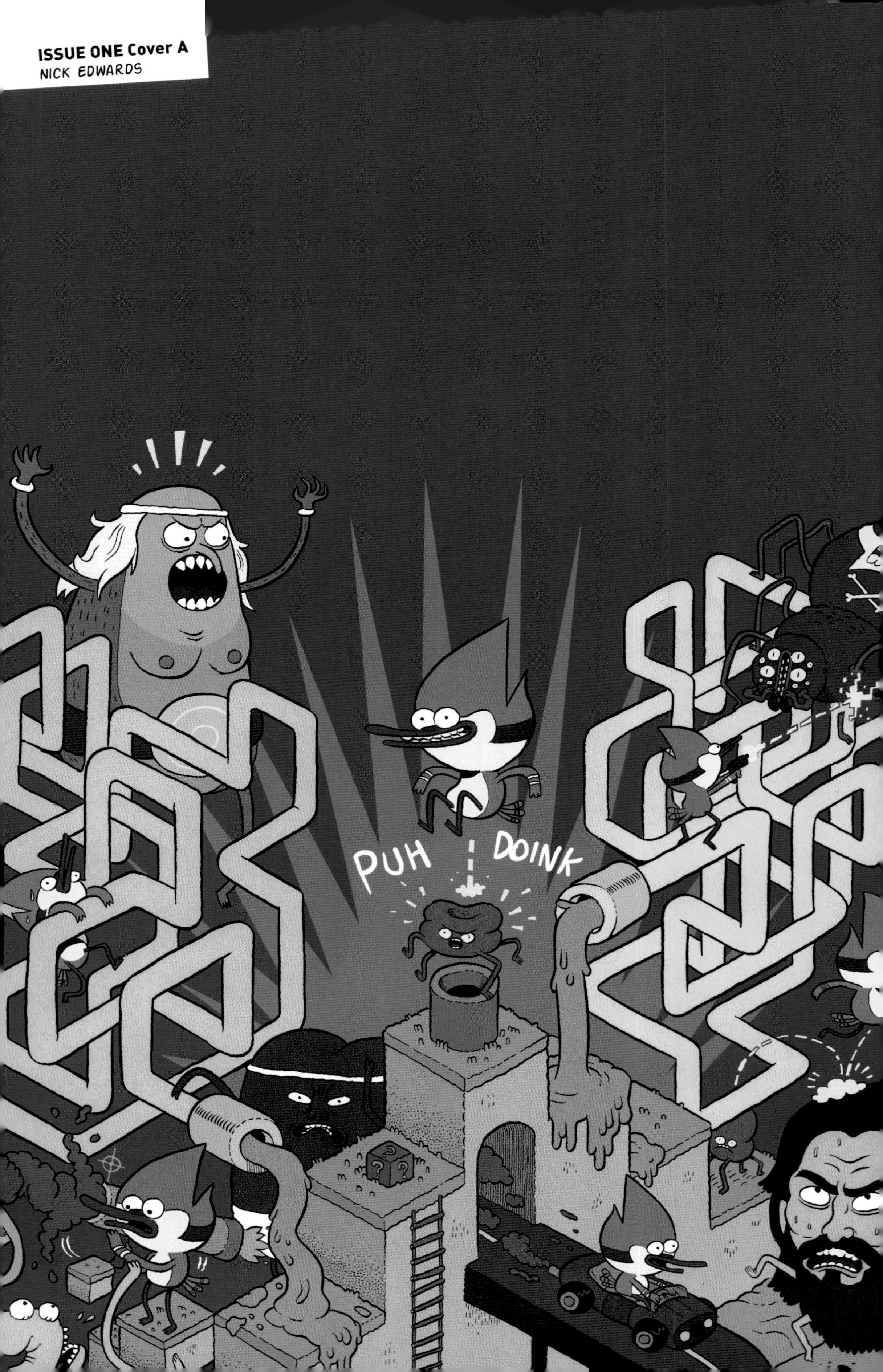

ISSUE TWO Cover B
NATHAN FOX
COLORS BY LOGAN FAERBER

ISSUE ONE Cover D
JOHN ALLISON
COLORS BY JOANNA ESTEP

TINDER

MORDECAI

ISSUE ONE Cover G
DUSTIN NGUYEN

REGULAR SHOW™

kaboom!

RIGBY

SKIPS

CART

POPS

MUSCLE MAN

BENSON

HI FIVE GHOST

ISSUE ONE Second Print
PHIL JACOBSON

ISSUE ONE Cards, Comics & Collectibles Cover
KATIE MᶜDERMOTT

ISSUE ONE Third Eye Comics Exclusive
JOSCELINE FENTON

ISSUE ONE
Dynamic Forces Exclusive
REBECCA CLEMENTS

ISSUE ONE Awesome Cons Exclusive
JERRY GAYLORD
COLORS BY LAUREN AFFE

ISSUE ONE San Diego
Comic-Con Exclusive
SINA GRACE
COLORS BY SHAUN STEVEN STRUBLE

ISSUE TWO Cover D
BRIAN BUTLER

ISSUE FOUR Cover C
JOE EISMA

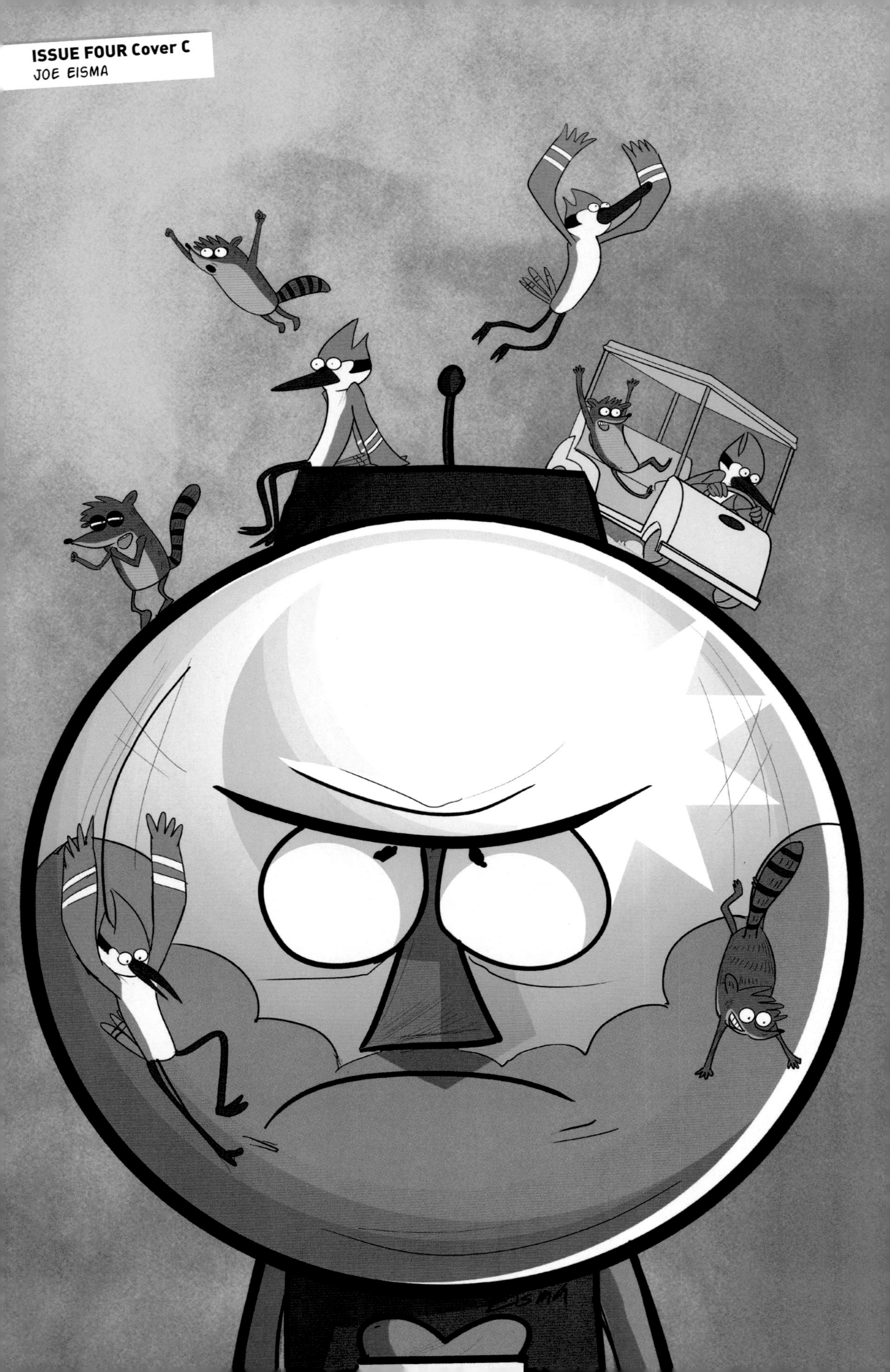

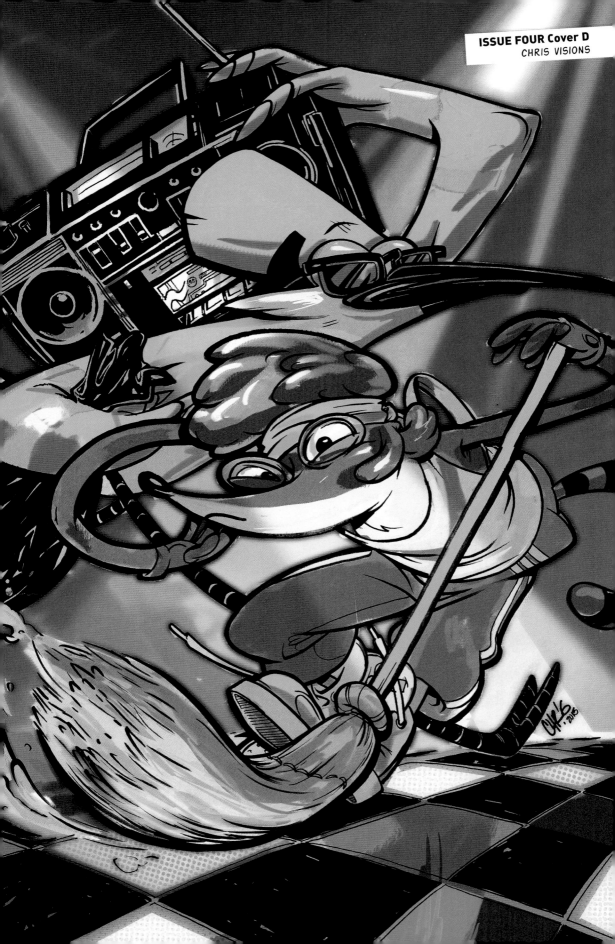

ISSUE FIVE Cover D
JAMES THE STANTON